Dancing

Published in collaboration with the
Imperial Society of Teachers of Dancing

Dancing

Foreword

This is the fourth book which the Imperial Society has prepared for the 'Know the Game' series. Hitherto each book has concentrated on one particular style and the most successful book has been that on Modern Ballroom Dancing which has sold over 145,000 copies.

During the past decade the Latin dances have become extremely popular and this new book describes the five dances most likely to be played at social functions. With the help of the photographs it should be possible for anyone to learn the basic steps and when these have been enjoyed and more knowledge is sought the Secretary of the Society will gladly put you in touch with a teacher of dancing who can help you.

Apart from being a most pleasant social pastime, advanced Ballroom Dancing can be a stimulating recreation and sport. International competitions now include couples from Australia, Japan, South Africa, the United States of America and about twenty other countries. Hundreds of thousands of people of many nations enjoy the movement and artistry of what is now known as the 'International Style' of ballroom dancing.

To reach a high standard of dancing it is advisable to enter for the various examinations and proficiency tests which the Imperial Society of Teachers of Dancing organise in schools of dancing throughout the country. These examinations provide an impartial assessment of the candidates' proficiency and encourage the attainment of good style and high standards.

The Society's Headquarters are at 70 Gloucester Place, London W.1, where a staff are in daily attendance to answer enquiries regarding the numerous activities of the Society and to advise prospective candidates for examination.

Alex Moore

Chairman,
Imperial Society of Teachers of Dancing.

Introduction

Ballroom dancing has no equal as a mental and physical recreation for people of all ages. The young and energetic will find that proficiency in what is now universally known as the 'International Style' will give them exercise, poise and balance which will prove of the utmost value in their pursuance of such sports as Golf, Tennis, Cricket and Football. In fact many of the leading players of these sports consider serious Ballroom Dancing an essential part of their training.

Ballroom Dancing is equally valuable to those busy people who require mental relaxation and an agreeable physical exercise that is not too strenuous. A reasonable standard of efficiency can be reached in a comparatively short time and it is necessary to learn only a few simple figures in each dance to enjoy the rhythmic pleasure that dancing can give.

Before attempting to learn the basic figures of any of the dances described in this book it is essential for the beginner to learn something about poise and how to walk correctly with a partner. This is dealt with on page 5. Study the notes and the illustrations very carefully and then try to dance a few walking steps forward and backward, first alone and then with a partner. This should be practised without music and then, after studying the notes on Rhythm on page 8, the steps could be practised with music.

Try to get into your mind at once that to walk with a partner in a ballroom is little more difficult than walking in the street. Most men are usually nervous about treading on their partner's feet, and consequently either push their feet along the floor (a fault which prevents a free movement) or they 'spreadeagle' their feet in a clumsy but gallant effort to avoid the feet of their partner. Always remember that if the poise of the body is correct, with the weight forward, the Lady will be taken along with you. Only if you dance with your weight back and hold your partner so tightly that she cannot escape will there be danger of treading on her toes.

To walk backwards is less natural and more difficult and requires far more practice. Again, if the poise of the body is correct, the action of the backward walk will be acquired more easily.

Now turn to the next page and make a start. It will lead you to many happy hours of pleasure.

The Poise and the Walk

Man

A natural walking step is the basis of ballroom dancing and to accomplish this with a free and flowing movement it is essential that the poise of the body is correct.

Stand in an upright position with the feet together. The body should be slightly braced at the waist without raising the shoulders. Take a fairly deep breath and this will give you an idea of the required position. Legs must be straight but not rigid. Knees will be very lightly flexed.

Now incline the body forward from the feet upwards until the weight is mainly over the balls of the feet.

Take the weight on to the right foot and step forward with a natural walking movement with the left foot. If the poise and distribution of the weight are correct, the left foot will commence to move forward with the ball of the foot in contact with the floor. As it passes the right foot, swing the left foot forward in the normal way and place it heel first and then on to the whole foot. The right heel will leave the floor as the left foot moves forward.

The feet must be quite straight. Practise walking on a straight line with the insides of the feet brushing past each other on every step.

Practise walking four steps forward and then four steps backward, but remember the Man must still keep his poise forward even when moving back. Never look downwards.

Lady

Stand in an upright position, but with the head and shoulders poised very slightly back. It is inadvisable for the beginner to allow the weight to move back, so endeavour to keep the weight over the balls of the feet even though the poise of the body is back.

To walk backward is far more difficult than to walk forward. A preliminary exercise of swinging the legs forward and backward from the hips while maintaining a good upright poise will be found helpful.

Now take the weight on to the left foot and move the right foot back with first the ball of the foot and then the toes skimming over the floor. At the full extent of the stride when the weight is taken on to the ball of the right foot, the ball of the left foot will gradually leave the floor and the weight will be central between the ball of the right foot and heel of the left foot. Lower the right heel slowly as the left foot is brought back with a little pressure on the heel. When it reaches the right foot the ball of the left foot must be in contact with the floor as it continues to move backward for another walk.

Remember that as a step is commenced the knees are slightly flexed, but not really bent. At the full extent of the stride the legs are straight but not rigid.

Keep the feet straight and practise four walks backward and forward. Keep the head to the left, looking over the Man's right shoulder. Never look down towards the feet. This will completely upset the balance.

The Hold

Man

Even if you are not a good dancer, you can always look smart on a ballroom floor if you have good poise and a correct hold.

Study the photographs and then stand with your partner and pay attention to the following points:

1. The left arm should slope slightly downwards from the shoulder to the elbow to avoid raising the shoulder. **Keep** this part of the arm well back. A common fault is to move the elbow forward, thus destroying the smart line.

2. Bend the arm quite sharply at the elbow. The forearm is held so that it is pointing upwards and slightly forward from the elbow.

3. Take the fingers of the Lady's right hand between the thumb and the first finger and hold the Lady's hand firmly but not tightly. The palm of the Man's left hand should face diagonally towards the floor in a forward direction. It must never be turned so that the palm is upwards. Avoid any tendency to drop the left hand lower than the wrist. The knuckles of the left hand should be kept slightly higher than the wrist.

4. The right hand is placed on the Lady's back between her left shoulder-blade and her waist. The forearm should slope downwards. This will enable the Man to keep his right elbow up. One of the worst faults is to drop the right elbow when holding the Lady.

This weakens the leads given by the Man when dancing and gives the Lady no support.

5. In Waltz, Quickstep and Slow Rhythm the Lady will stand very slightly to the Man's right side. The couple should be in contact with each other from the hips upward. This is most important as when the Man wishes to lead the Lady into any turning movements she must take her lead from the movement of the Man's body rather than from any conscious 'push or pull' with his right or left hand.

Practise the four walks forward and backward with a partner and endeavour to acquire a firm and smart hold while moving. Practise until the walks can be danced with ease and without losing contact with your partner.

Lady

The Lady's hold will always depend to some extent upon the Man. She must always adapt her hold to the requirements of the Man even if his hold is not correct.

Adopt the poise described on the previous page and stand in front of the Man, very slightly to his right side. Study the illustrations and then watch the following points:—

1. Raise the right hand with the fingers held close together and allow the Man to take it to his normal position. He should hold the fingers of the Lady's right hand. The Lady will then close her thumb over the thumb of his left hand. The palms of the two hands will be touching lightly.

2. The right arm may slope slightly downwards from the shoulder to the elbow and then upwards from the elbow to meet the Man's left hand. Do not lift the right elbow too high as this will force the Man's hand back and disturb his normal hold. Also avoid hanging on to his hand and pulling it downwards. If the body is braced slightly at the waist this heavy pulling on the Man's left hand is more easily avoided.

3. The left hand is placed comfortably on the Man's right arm near his shoulder. Group the fingers neatly and do not keep them rigid. Allow the left forearm to rest lightly on the Man's right arm but avoid bearing downwards. If the poise of the Lady is correct there will be less tendency to lean heavily on the Man.

Remember that good poise and balance will help to keep you in contact with your partner. Never pull yourself towards your partner with your right or left hand.

Rhythm

Everyone has a sense of rhythm and it is quite easy to develop it sufficiently to dance to music. Listen to a band playing a bright march. A repetition of two beats is heard, one of which is stronger than the other. It seems to invite you to count 1.2, 1.2, 1.2, 1.2, with a strong accent on the first beat. Here are some helpful hints on the rhythm of the dances dealt with in this book.

Waltz

Waltz music should be played at 30-32 bars a minute and each bar of music has three beats (3 crotchets). The first beat of each bar is accented. You should take one step to each beat of music and make sure that your first step, usually a step forward or backward, is taken on the first beat which is always accented.

Quickstep

Quickstep music should be played at 46-48 bars a minute although it is advisable to try the steps to a slower tempo at first. There are four beats in each bar of music and it will be noticed that there is a stronger accent on the first and third beats in each bar. When you take a slow step your foot is placed on the floor on the first beat, the other foot is commencing to move during the second beat. Take the next step on the third beat, and the other foot is commencing to move during the fourth beat. When you dance a quick chassé movement you count 'Quick, Quick' and take two steps in the time of one Slow step.

Slow Rhythm (Social Foxtrot)

The music is played at about 26-34 bars a minute. As in the Quickstep there are four beats in each bar of music and the value of each 'Slow' and 'Quick' is the same as in the Quickstep. Two beats are given to each 'Slow' and one beat each to a count of 'Quick, Quick'.

Cha Cha Cha

Cha Cha Cha music is played at about 30-34 bars a minute. As in the Quickstep and Slow Rhythm there are four beats in each bar of music but five steps are danced to these four beats to the count of '1, 2, 3 & 4'. The first two steps have one beat each, the third and fourth steps only a half a beat each as this beat is 'split', while the fifth step has one beat. When you are dancing it is helpful to say 'Step, Step, Cha Cha Cha'.

Owing to the complexities of the Latin American rhythms you will sometimes hear the 'Cha Cha Cha' occurring on the first and fourth beats of the music, so advanced dancers will take their first step on the second beat, counting '2, 3, 4 & 1'.

Samba

The music is played at about 48-56 bars a minute and there are two beats to the bar. The Basic Movement is counted 'Slow, Slow' and there is one beat for each step. In some figures we have to fit three steps into one bar of music so we split the first beat and count 'Slow a Slow'. The first step has three quarters of a beat, the second step a quarter beat and the third step a whole beat.

The 'Line of Dance'

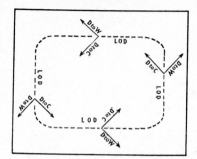

L.O.D. =
Line of Dance.

D. to C. =
Diagonally to Centre.

D. to W. =
Diagonally to Wall.

When you dance in a ballroom, you move round the room in an anti-clockwise direction. When reading descriptions of the figures it is important to remember that there are four 'Lines of Dance' in the room.

If you stand at the side of the room with your right shoulder nearest to the wall, the 'Line of Dance' is directly in front of you. This will apply whichever side or end of the room you are standing—or dancing.

If you turn half right you will be facing diagonally to the wall. If you turn half left, you will be facing diagonally to the centre. Note that 'centre' is not the actual centre of the room, but an imaginary line running parallel to the wall on the left side of the dancer when he is facing the Line of Dance.

The illustration on this page will help you to understand this important point.

The Waltz

The Waltz is usually the first dance the beginner wants to learn. There is one step to each beat of the music. When listening to Waltz music it will be noticed that there is a slightly stronger accent on the first of each three beats, and the first step of each figure is taken on this strong beat.

In most basic figures the first step is a strong step forward or backward; the second step is a side step and the feet are closed for the third step.

Learn the Closed Change first and practise this moving in a forward direction around the room starting with alternate feet, see pages 10 and 11.

After the Natural and Reverse Turns have been learned the three figures are amalgamated in this way :—

1. Dance a Closed Change commencing with left foot and facing diagonally to the wall.
2. Dance a complete Natural Turn, commencing diagonally to the wall and ending facing diagonally to the centre.
3. Dance a Closed Change commencing with right foot and facing diagonally to the centre.
4. Dance a complete Reverse Turn, commencing diagonally to the centre and ending facing diagonally to the wall.

Now repeat the amalgamation from the beginning. At a corner a series of Natural Turns may be used. Whenever a turn is to be made give a good swing forward or backward as the first step is taken. The first step is taken with a slight relaxing of the knee. Commence to rise at the end of the first of each **three** steps and then continue to rise gradually on the second and third steps. Lower at the end of the third step.

The Waltz—The Closed Change

R.F. = Right Foot
L.F. = Left Foot

Start here

Man

Reading from left to right the illustrations show the Closed Change step, one of the most simple and popular figures in the Waltz, danced first with the Man commencing with the left foot, and then with the right foot. Dance it straight down the room at first.

1. L.F. forward. **Man.**
1. R.F. back. **Lady.**

2. R.F. to side and slightly forward.
2. L.F. to side and slightly back.

3. Close L.F. to R.F.
3. Close R.F. to L.F.

The Man takes the first step heel first. The second and third steps are taken on the toes. He lowers the left heel lightly as the right foot steps forward to repeat the figure with right foot.

Lady

The Lady lowers the right heel on step one and rises to the toes on two and three. She will lower the right heel as the **left** foot moves back to repeat the figure. The Lady dances the figure moving backward, first commencing with the right foot.

4. **R.F. forward.**
4. L.F. back.

5. **L.F. to side and slightly forward.**
5. R.F. to side and slightly back.

6. **Close R.F. to L.F.**
6. Close L.F. to R.F.

The Waltz—The Natural Turn

Man

The Natural Turn consists of six steps and three-quarters of a turn to right is made on these steps. Start facing diagonally to the wall and end facing diagonally to the centre.

Until the Reverse Turn has been learnt, follow the Natural Turn with a Closed Change commencing with right foot and turning slightly to the right. Follow with one or more Closed Changes before you repeat the Natural Turn.

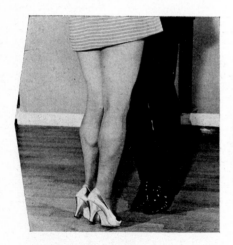  

6. Close L.F. to R.F.

6. Still turning close R.F. to L.F.

5. R.F. to side, Right toe pointing diagonally to centre.

5. L.F. to side backing towards centre.

4. L.F. back turning to Right.

4. R.F. forward turning to Right.

Lady

The Natural Turn consists of six steps and three-quarters of a turn to right is made on these steps. Start with back diagonally to the wall and end backing diagonally to the centre, then dance several Closed Changes before repeating the Turn. On the Closed Change following the Natural Turn make a slight turn to the right.

Follow the steps as shown in the illustrations but remember also to follow your partner.

Start here

3. **Close R.F. to L.F. Now backing the Line of Dance.**
3. Close L.F. to R.F. Now facing the Line of Dance.

2. **L.F. to side, body backing diagonally to centre.**
2. R.F. to side, Right toe pointing to Line of Dance.

1. R.F. forward, turning to right **Man**

1. L.F. back, turning to Right. **Lady**

The Waltz—The Reverse Turn

Man

The steps of the Reverse Turn are practically the same as those of the Natural Turn. In the Reverse Turn, start facing diagonally to the centre and end facing diagonally to the wall.

When sure of the steps turn back to page 9 and try to amalgamate the three figures: The Closed Change, Natural Turn and Reverse Turn.

Start here

Man 1. L.F. forward, turning to left.

Lady 1. R.F. back, turning to left.

2. R.F. to side, body backing diagonally to wall.
2. L.F. to side, Left toe pointing to Line of Dance.

3. Close L.F. to R.F. Now backing Line of Dance.
3. Close R.F. to L.F. Now facing Line of Dance.

Lady

The steps of the Reverse Turn are practically the same as those of the Natural Turn. Lady will commence the Reverse Turn backing diagonally to the centre and end it backing diagonally to the wall. The correct way of amalgamating the Closed Change, Natural Turn and Reverse Turn is given on page 9.

4. R.F. back, turning to Left.

4. L.F. forward, turning to Left.

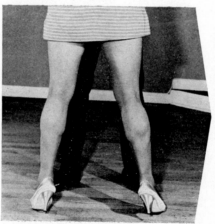

5. L.F. to side, Left toe pointing diagonally to wall.

5. R.F. to side, body backing towards wall.

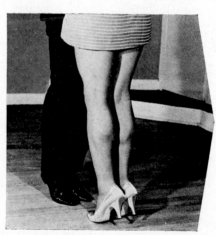

6. Close R.F. to L.F. Now facing diagonally to wall.

6. Still turning, close L.F. to R.F.

The Waltz—The Natural Spin Turn

Man

This delightful figure consists of the first three steps of a Natural Turn followed by a spinning movement of three steps. After the sixth step of the Spin the Man will step back on the right foot, diagonally to the centre and dance steps 4,5,6 of a Reverse Turn. Follow this with a Closed Change danced diagonally to the wall, and then a Natural Turn. Commence facing diagonally to wall.

6. L.F. to side and slightly back, backing diagonally to centre. (Toes, then lower Heel).

6 Turn on ball of L.F. and brush R.F. to L.F., then step diagonally forward with R.F. (Toes, then lower).

5. Take weight forward to R.F. down the Line of Dance. (Heel). Still turning to Right.

5. Move L.F. back and leftwards. Now backing the Line of Dance. Still turning to Right.

4. L.F. back and pivot a half turn to Right. Keep R.F. forward. Turn on ball of L.F.

4. R.F. forward and turn strongly to Right. Step on heel then turn on ball of foot.

Lady

The Natural Spin Turn consists of the first three steps of a Natural Turn followed by a spinning movement of three steps. The Lady's steps differ slightly from those of the Man, and the Lady must always follow the Man regarding the exact amount of turn to be made.

After dancing the Spin, step forward on the left foot and dance steps 4,5,6 of a Reverse Turn. Commence backing diagonally to wall.

Start here

3. Close R.F. to L.F. Now backing the Line of Dance.
3. Close L.F. to R.F. Now facing the Line of Dance.

2. L.F. to side, body backing diagonally to centre.
2. R.F. to side, Right toe pointing to Line of Dance.

1. R.F. forward, turning to Right.
Man
1. L.F. back, turning to Right.
Lady

The Quickstep

The Quickstep is undoubtedly the most popular dance in the ballroom today. The music is bright and few people can resist the appeal of a rhythmic Quickstep tune.

The dance consists of walking steps and a movement called a Chassé. This Chassé movement is taken quickly and in some ways resembles the movement used to change step when marching.

To understand this quick change of rhythm, try walking along the room counting 'Left, Right, Left, Right'. Now do a quick change of step 'Left-Right-Left' as is used when marching and continue walking to the count of 'Right, Left, Right, Left'. Follow this with another quick change of step 'Right-Left-Right' and continue from the beginning. In the change of step the feet are closed on the second step.

If instead of counting 'Left, Right' you count the full sequence of steps 'Slow, Slow, Slow, Slow', 'Quick-Quick-Slow', 'Slow, Slow, Slow, Slow', 'Quick-Quick-Slow', you are using the type of rhythmic count which is used in dancing.

In the Quickstep, a 'Slow' count occupies two beats, and 'Quick' counts have one beat each.

Before learning any of the basic steps practise walking alone, and then with a partner as described on pages 4 and 5. When this has been mastered it is advisable to learn to dance a Chassé as described on the facing page.

When you can dance the Chassé turn to page 20 and learn the Quarter Turns and then the Natural Turn, following these with the Chassé Reverse Turn, the Progressive Chassé and Forward Lock. Simple methods of amalgamating these figures as you learn them are given below.

1. Dance a few walking steps and then the Quarter Turns commencing with the right foot. The Quarter Turns can then be repeated at once or if near a corner step forward with the right foot into a Natural Turn to get round the corner. Repeat along the next side of the room.

2. Dance the Quarter Turns and then go straight into the Natural Turn with the extra 'Slow' step as explained in the chart. Follow this with the Chassé Reverse Turn, the last step of the Natural Turn becoming the first step of the Chassé Reverse Turn. Now go into the Quarter Turns or a Natural Turn if near a corner.

3. Dance steps 1 to 4 of the Quarter Turns and then step back with the right foot into the Progressive Chassé and Forward Lock. Follow with the Quarter Turns or the Natural Turn. (The last step of the Forward Lock will become the first step of these two figures and therefore will be outside the Lady on her right side.) The Progressive Chassé and Forward Lock can be danced directly following the third step of the Chassé Reverse Turn, in which case the first step of the Progressive Chassé will be taken straight back down the Line of Dance.

The Chassé

Here is a simple exercise to help you to understand how to dance a Chassé. Commence facing the wall and keep facing the wall throughout, so that you are moving sideways along the room.

Keep repeating this round the room until you can dance it fairly quickly, using the rhythmic count given below. This exercise can be practised by both the Man and the Lady as it is only a preliminary exercise. The foot diagrams below will help you. The white foot is the right foot and the black foot is the left.

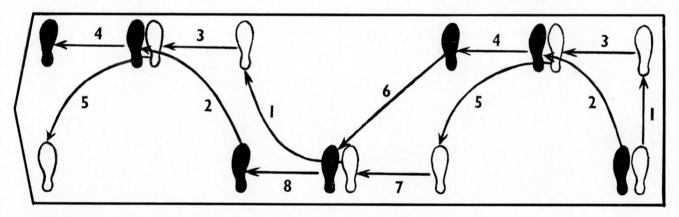

Start here

Now repeat the Chassé commencing with a step backwards.

The steps are :—

5. R.F. back.	Slow (Toes, then lower Heel).	
6. L.F. to side.	Quick (Toes).	
7. Close R.F. to L.F.	Quick (Toes).	
8. L.F. to side.	Slow (Toes, then lower Heel).	

1. R.F. forward.	Slow (Heel).	
2. L.F. to side.	Quick (Toes).	
3. Close R.F. to L.F.	Quick (Toes).	
4. L.F. to side.	Slow (Toes, then lower Heel).	

The Quickstep—The Quarter Turns
Man

This is the most useful figure in the Quickstep, as it enables the couple to progress along the room. It consists of a Chassé turning to the right and then a compact type of Chassé called a Heel Pivot which turns to the left.

After stepping forward on the heel for first step, take the next three steps on the toes. The Heel Pivot is danced with the feet almost flat. Commence facing diagonally to wall.

8. L.F. forward diagonally to wall. (Slow).

8. R.F. back, diagonally to wall. (Slow).

7. Complete the turn to Left to face diagonally to wall. (Quick).

7. Close L.F. to R.F. turning to back diagonally to wall. (Quick).

6. Close L.F. to R.F., commencing to turn to Left on right heel. (Quick).

6. R.F. to side, body facing centre. (Quick).

5. R.F. back diagonally to centre, turning to Left. (Slow).

5. L.F. forward turning to Left. (Slow).

Lady

This important figure enables the couple to progress along the room, first turning to the right with a Chassé and then the Lady also uses a Chassé to turn to the left while the Man dances a more compact Heel Pivot.

After the first step back, the next three steps are taken on the toes. The fifth step is taken forward on the heel. Dance steps six and seven on the toes and then lower for a normal step backward. Commence backing diagonally to wall.

Start here

4. L.F. to side and slightly back. (Slow).

4. R.F. diagonally forward, slightly between Man's feet. (Slow).

3. Close R.F. to L.F. Now backing diagonally to centre. (Quick).

3. Close L.F. to R.F. Now facing diagonally to centre. (Quick).

2. L.F. to side, body facing wall. (Quick).

2. R.F. to side, body facing centre. (Quick).

1. R.F. forward, turning to Right. (Slow). **Man**

1. L.F. back, turning to Right. (Slow). **Lady**

21

The Quickstep—The Natural Turn

Man

After dancing the Quarter Turns along the side of the room, the Natural Turn can be used to turn the corner. It consists of a Chassé turning to right, followed by a turn on the left heel with the feet almost together. Steps two and three are taken on the toes. Commence facing diagonally to wall. This figure may also be danced along the side of the room making step '5' a little wider, then close L.F. to R.F. without weight counting 'Slow'. You are now facing diagonally to centre ready to go straight into the Chassé Reverse Turn overleaf.

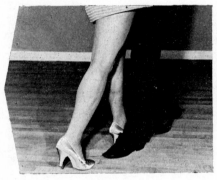  

6. L.F. forward, diagonally to wall of next Line of Dance. (Slow).

6. Brush R.F. past L.F. and step back with R.F. diagonally to wall of next Line of Dance. (Slow).

5. Turn on left heel to face diagonally to wall of next Line of Dance and close R.F. near L.F. (Slow).

5. L.F. to side across front of partner. Now backing to next Line of Dance. (Slow).

4. L.F. back, turning to the Right. (Slow).

4. R.F. forward, turning to Right. (Slow).

Lady

This figure is used to turn corners. It consists of a Chassé turning to the right, and then an open type of turn where the right foot brushes past the left foot instead of closing. Steps two and three are taken on the toes. After stepping forward on the heel for the fourth step the fifth step is taken on the ball of foot but there is no rise. Commence backing diagonally to wall. It may also be danced along the side of the room taking step '5' backing diagonally to centre and then closing R.F. to L.F. without weight counting 'Slow'. Now go straight into the Chassé Reverse Turn overleaf.

Start here

3. Close R.F. to L.F. turning to back the Line of Dance near a corner. (Quick).

2. L.F. to side, body backing diagonally to centre. (Quick).

1. R.F. forward turning to Right. (Slow). **Man**

3. Close L.F. to R.F. Now facing the Line of Dance. (Quick)

2. R.F. to side, with Right toe pointing to Line of Dance. (Quick).

1. L.F. back, turning to Right. (Slow). **Lady**

The Quickstep—The Chassé Reverse Turn

Man

This Reverse Turn is the easiest for the beginner to learn. It consists of a Chassé turning to the left and then the last four steps of the Quarter Turns. It can be taken directly following the Natural Turn danced along the side of the room.

Steps two and three only are taken on the toes. Commence facing diagonally to the centre.

Start here

Man 1. L.F. forward, turning to Left. (Slow).

Lady 1. R.F. back, turning to Left. (Slow).

2. R.F. to side, backing diagonally to wall. (Quick).

2. L.F. to side, Left toe pointing to Line of Dance. (Quick).

3. Close L.F. to R.F. turning to back the line of Dance. (Quick).

3. Close R.F. to L.F. Now facing Line of Dance. (Quick).

Lady

This is the easiest Reverse Turn for the beginner to learn. It consists of Chassé turns, turning to the left on each. The first three steps are similar to the Natural Turn but danced turning to the left, and the last four steps are the same as the last four steps of the Quarter Turns.

Steps two, three, five and six are taken on the toes. Commence backing diagonally to centre.

Steps 5, 6, and 7 are the "heel pivot" shown in steps 6, 7, and 8 of the quarter turns on page 20.

4. R.F. back, turning to Left. (Slow).

4. L.F. forward, turning to Left. (Slow).

5. Close L.F. to R.F., commencing to turn to Left on Right heel. (Quick).

5. R.F. to side, facing centre. (Quick).

6. Continue turning to Left to face diagonally to wall. (Quick).

6. Close L.F. to R.F. turning to back diagonally to wall. (Quick).

7. L.F. forward, diagonally to wall. (Slow).

7. R.F. back diagonally to wall. (Slow).

The Quickstep—The Progressive Chassé and Forward Lock

Man

These are very popular figures in the Quickstep consisting of a Chassé turning to the left and then a type of Chassé movement danced forward taking the first and last steps outside the Lady on her right side and crossing the foot behind instead of closing. Care must be taken to keep contact with the Lady when stepping outside. Dance these figures after the first four steps of the Quarter Turns or the first three of the Chassé Reverse Turn.

After the first step back the next three steps are taken on the toes. The fifth step is taken forward on the heel and steps six, seven and eight are on the toes, lowering and stepping forward on the heel on nine.

To learn the figures commence backing diagonally to the centre.

9. R.F. forward, outside Lady on her right side, facing diagonally to the wall. (Slow).

9. L.F. back, Man outside on right side, backing diagonally to the wall. (Slow).

8. L.F. diagonally forward, facing diagonally to the wall. (Slow).

8. R.F. diagonally back, backing diagonally to the wall. (Slow).

7. Cross R.F. behind L.F. still facing diagonally to the wall. (Quick).

7. Cross L.F. in front of R.F. still backing diagonally to the wall. (Quick).

6. L.F. diagonally forward, facing diagonally to the wall. (Quick).

6. R.F. back, backing diagonally to the wall. (Quick).

26

Lady

These popular figures consist of a Chassé turning to the left and then a type of Chassé moving backwards and crossing in front instead of closing. After stepping forward on the heel for step one take the next three steps on the toes and then lower for a normal backward step. Steps six, seven and eight are on the toes and then lower again for a normal step back. Commence facing diagonally to the centre.

Start here

5. R.F. forward outside Lady on her right side, facing diagonally to the wall. (Slow).

4. L.F. to side and slightly forward, facing diagonally to the wall. (Slow).

3. Close R.F. to L.F., now facing diagonally to the wall. (Quick).

2. L.F. to side, Left toe pointing diagonally to the wall. (Quick).

1. R.F. back **Man** turning to Left. (Slow).

5. L.F. back, Man outside on right side, backing diagonally to the wall. (Slow).

4. R.F. to side and slightly back, backing diagonally to the wall. (Slow).

3. Close L.F. to R.F., now backing diagonally to the wall. (Quick).

2. R.F. to side, body backing the wall. (Quick).

1. L.F. forward, **Lady** turning to Left. (Slow).

27

Slow Rhythm (Social Foxtrot)

The beginner who has studied the earlier pages of this book will have noticed that one of the characteristics of the Waltz and Quickstep is a free and flowing movement with the use of long steps. However, he will discover that at social or public dances the floor is usually so crowded or small that it is impossible to give the dances the free, rhythmic interpretation which is the aim of all who love to dance well. Such surroundings call for a rather different form of dancing known as 'Rhythm' dancing. This is possibly the easiest and most useful dance for the beginner to learn and it may also be danced to Quickstep music when the occasion demands.

The figures consist of two walking steps forward or back counted 'Slow, Slow' and a step to the side and a close counted 'Quick, Quick'. This rhythm of two slows and two quicks is constant throughout the dance, the Man starting every figure with his left foot and the Lady with her right foot.

The steps are quite small and no attempt should be made to use long steps and flowing movement. All the steps are taken flat—there is no rise to the toes. Try to acquire a soft flexing of the knees to give the dance rhythmic expression. As you practise say 'Step, Stop, Step, Stop, Side, Close' as follows :—
Rhythm of steps . . .

	1. SLOW	2. SLOW	3. QUICK	4. QUICK
Say . . .	'Step, Stop'	'Step, Stop'	'Side'	'Close'

The hold is similar to the Waltz and Quickstep but is a little more compact as will be seen by the photograph, the Man placing his right arm further round the Lady slightly above her waist with the left forearm drawn very slightly inwards towards the head.

Here is a simple exercise to help you with the figures. Face the wall and take two forward steps. L.F. (Slow), R.F. (Slow). Now step to the side with L.F. (Quick) and close R.F. to L.F. (Quick). Now take two steps back L.F. (Slow), R.F. (Slow), then step to the side with L.F. (Quick) and close R.F. to L.F. (Quick). Repeat this exercise facing the wall throughout so that you are moving sideways along the room. The Lady will commence backing the wall and take two backward steps, R.F. (Slow), L.F. (Slow), then R.F. to side (Quick) and close L.F. to R.F. (Quick). Then two forward steps R.F. (Slow), L.F. (Slow), side R.F. (Quick) and close L.F. to R.F. (Quick).

Practise this exercise first and when you can do the steps quite easily turn to page 30 and learn the Quarter Turn to Right and the Quarter Turn to Left. You will find the steps are the same as those in the practise exercise but you will be making a little turn. Next turn to the Right Rock Turn and then the Side Step.

Simple methods of amalgamating the figures as you learn them are given below.

1. Dance the Quarter Turn to the Right and follow immediately with the Quarter Turn to the Left. Repeat these two figures as often as you wish.

2. After the Quarter Turn to Right you are backing diagonally to the centre. Now step back with the L.F. into the Right Rock Turn. Repeat the Right Rock Turn four times making a quarter of a turn on each one until you are backing diagonally to the centre again. Now step L.F. back into the Quarter Turn to Left. Remember you may repeat the Right Rock Turn as often as you wish. According to the amount you turn you may need to do more or less repetitions. If you are near a corner you will not need to repeat the Right Rock Turn so often— three repetitions should be sufficient for you to end backing diagonally to the centre of the next line of dance, then step back as before into the Quarter Turn to Left.

3. Dance the Quarter Turn to Right and the Quarter Turn to Left. Make a little less turn on the last two steps to end facing the wall. Now go into the Side Step and repeat this two or three times. Turn slightly to the right on the last two steps to back diagonally

to the centre and continue by stepping back on the L.F. into the Quarter Turn to Left.

The Hold

Slow Rhythm—The Quarter Turns to Right and Left

Man

These are the most popular figures in Slow Rhythm dancing. They consist of two forward steps and a 'side, close' turning a quarter to the right, then two backward steps and a 'side, close' turning a quarter to the left, using a similar pattern to the Quarter Turns in the Quickstep. Dance the Quarter Turn to Right immediately followed by the Quarter Turn to Left as shown in the

The Quarter Turn to Left

Start here

4. Close R.F. to L.F. facing diagonally to the wall. (Quick).

4. Close L.F. to R.F. backing diagonally to the wall. (Quick).

3. L.F. to side, small step, left toe pointing diagonally to the wall. (Quick).

3. R.F. to side, backing diagonally to the wall. (Quick).

2. R.F. back turning to left. (Slow).

2. L.F. forward turning to left. (Slow).

1. L.F. back, backing diagonally to the centre. (Slow). **Man**

1. R.F. forward, facing diagonally to centre. (Slow). **Lady**

30

photographs. Commence the Quarter Turn to Right facing diagonally to the wall and the Quarter Turn to Left backing diagonally to the centre.

The Quarter Turn to Right

Lady

The Quarter Turns are the most popular figures in this dance. The Quarter Turn to Right is commenced backing diagonally to the wall and consists of two backward steps and a 'side, close'. The Quarter Turn to Left commences facing diagonally to the centre and consists of two forward steps and a 'side, close'.

Start here

4. Close R.F. to L.F. backing diagonally to the centre. (Quick).

4. Close L.F. to R.F. facing diagonally to the centre. (Quick).

3. L.F. to side, backing diagonally to centre. (Quick).

3. R.F. to side, small step, right toe pointing diagonally to centre. (Quick).

2. R.F. forward, turning to right. (Slow).

2. L.F. back, turning to right. (Slow).

1. L.F. forward, facing diagonally to wall. (Slow). **Man**

1. R.F. back, backing diagonally to wall. (Slow). **Lady**

Slow Rhythm—The Right Rock Turn

This figure is danced after the Quarter Turn to Left and may be used along the side of the room or to get round a corner. The Man dances a step back on L.F. and then rocks forward to R.F. while the Lady steps forward R.F. and rocks back on to L.F. This is followed with a 'side, close' turning to the right. It is helpful to say 'Step, Rock, Side, Close' while learning the figure. Repeat this Right Rock Turn four times making a quarter turn to right on each one to end backing diagonally to the centre again, then continue by stepping back with L.F. into the Quarter Turn to Left. Remember to commence backing (Lady facing) diagonally to the centre.

Start here

4. Close R.F. to L.F. backing diagonally to the wall. (Quick).	3. L.F. to side, backing diagonally to wall. (Quick).	2. Rock forward to R.F. turning to right. (Slow)	1. L.F. back, backing diagonally to centre. (Slow). **Man**
4. Close L.F. to R.F. facing diagonally to the wall. (Quick).	3. R.F. to side, small step, right toe pointing diagonally to the wall. (Quick).	2. Rock back to L.F. turning to right. (Slow).	1. R.F. forward, facing diagonally to centre. (Slow). **Lady**

Slow Rhythm—The Side Step

This is an attractive figure which is taken directly following the Quarter Turn to Left. Make less turn on the third and fourth steps of the latter to end facing the wall and then remain facing the wall throughout the Side Step. The steps of the Man and the Lady are similar. Repeat them two or three times and then make a slight turn to the right on steps three and four so that the Man will back and the Lady face diagonally to the centre. Continue by stepping back L.F. into the Quarter Turn to Left. Commence facing (Lady backing) the wall.

Start here

4. Close R.F. to L.F. (Quick).

4. Close L.F. to R.F. (Quick).

3. L.F. to side. (Quick).

3. R.F. to side. (Quick).

2. R.F. to side and move L.F. towards R.F. without weight. (Slow).

2. L.F. to side and move R.F. towards L.F. without weight. (Slow).

1. L.F. to side and move R.F. towards L.F. without weight. (Slow). **Man**

1. R.F. to side and move L.F. towards R.F. without weight. (Slow). **Lady**

KTG
Sequence Dancing

Produced in collaboration with the Imperial Society of Teachers of Dancing, this book illustrates nine of the most popular sequence dances, many arranged in recent years but including such old favourites as the Veleta and the Boston Two-Step.

With the aid of photographs and precise instructions the beginner will soon master and enjoy this most social and enjoyable pastime.

Size 5¼″ x 8″, 40 pages, fully illustrated, ISBN 0 7158 0208 0.

EP Publishing Limited, Bradford Road, East Ardsley, Wakefield, West Yorkshire, WF3 2JN.

The Hold and Poise (Cha Cha Cha and Samba)

The Man and Lady will stand in a naturally erect position directly opposite each other and about six inches apart. The Man will take the Lady's right hand in his left hand and raise the arm in a similar manner to the hold already described at the beginning of this book, but as you will see by the photographs his right hand will be placed a little higher on the Lady's back on her left shoulder blade. The Lady will rest her left hand lightly on the Man's shoulder.

   Study the photographs and then pay attention to the following points:

1. The Man should place his right hand quite firmly on the Lady's back but must allow her to keep her position taking care not to pull her towards him.

2. The Lady should try to press very slightly against the Man's right hand in order to maintain her position a little away from him.

3. Try to keep the body slightly braced at the waist and the shoulders relaxed.

4. Remember to keep your head up and resist the temptation to look down at the floor or at your partner's feet.

The Cha Cha Cha

The Cha Cha Cha is possibly the most popular of the Latin American dances and is almost always frequently included in the dance band's repertoire. The gay, rhythmic music sets everyone's toes tapping and it is certainly a dance the beginner wants to learn.

Unlike the dances previously described in this book the Cha Cha Cha does not move around the dance floor so therefore it does not matter which part of the room you are facing when you commence a figure.

The Chassé is an important part of each figure and consists of three steps. You have already learned to dance the Chassé in the Quickstep so you should have little trouble in mastering the Cha Cha Cha Chassé which is really the same except that on the second step the foot will only move towards the other foot instead of closing. It is called an 'Open Chassé' and here is a simple exercise to help you learn it:—

Chassé to the Left.

Stand with the feet together and the weight on the right foot.

		Say:
1. L.F. to side, small step	... ...	'Cha'
2. Move R.F. about half way towards L.F.	... ...	'Cha'
3. L.F. to side, small step	... ...	'Cha'

Chassé to the Right.

1. R.F. to side, small step	... ...	'Cha'
2. Move L.F. about half way towards R.F.	... ...	'Cha'
3. R.F. to side, small step	... ...	'Cha'

When you have mastered the Chassé practise the following exercise: Stand with the feet together and the weight on R.F. and mark time in place, first with L.F. and then with R.F. counting '1, 2', then Chassé to the Left for '3 & 4'. Now mark time in place, R.F., L.F., counting '1, 2' and Chassé to the Right for '3 & 4'. Repeat this several times saying '1, 2, 3 & 4' or 'Step, Step, Cha Cha Cha'. When you can do this quite easily turn to page 38 and learn the Basic Movement, then progress to the other figures.

Points to remember:

1. All the steps are quite small and you should never take a step forward on the heel. Try to take each step with the ball of the foot in contact with the floor, lowering the heel at the end of the step.

2. The hips should move in a supple and graceful manner although this is not always easy for the beginner to achieve. The hip movement takes place as the weight is transferred on to a foot, the hips

moving to the left as the weight is taken on to the left foot and to the right as the weight is taken on to the right foot. To feel this movement stand with your feet a little apart and imagine you are waiting for a bus. You feel a little tired so take your weight completely on to your left foot to rest the right one. You will feel your hips move over to the left. Now reverse the procedure taking your weight fully over to the right foot to rest the left foot. You should now feel your hips move over to the right. Try this several times and you will soon feel the hips moving quite freely. However, this hip movement should never be exaggerated.

Here are some simple ways to amalgamate the figures as you learn them:

1. Dance the Basic Movement several times. When you can do it quite easily try a gradual turn to the left. Make about a quarter turn on each Basic Movement.

2. Dance the Basic Movement and then follow the Basic Movement with the Lady's Solo Turn under arm. Having regained hold with the right hand continue with more Basic Movements.

3. Dance the Basic Movement and release hold with the right hand at the end of the last Chassé. Now turn to the right (Lady turns to the left) and continue into the New York. Repeat this figure once or twice more and then regain normal hold and step L.F. forward into the Basic Movement.

4. Again dance the Basic Movement but release hold with both hands as you dance the last Chassé. Now go straight into the Time Steps. Repeat these once or twice more and follow with the Basic Movement regaining normal hold.

Cha Cha Cha—Basic Movement

The steps for the Man and Lady are similar and you may repeat them as many times as you wish. When you can dance them easily try making a gradual turn to the left throughout the figure.

Start here

1. L.F. forward. (1)
Man

1. R.F. back. (1)
Lady

2. Replace weight back to R.F. (2)

2. Replace weight forward to L.F. (2)

3. L.F. to side, small step. (3)

3. R.F. to side, small step. (3)

4. Move R.F. very slightly towards L.F. (&)

4. Move L.F. very slightly towards R.F. (&)

5. L.F. to side, small step. (4)

5. R.F. to side, small step. (4)

6. R.F. back. (1)

6. L.F. forward. (1)

7. Replace weight forward to L.F. (2)

7. Replace weight back to R.F. (2)

8. R.F. to side, small step. (3)

8. L.F. to side, small step. (3)

9. Move L.F. very slightly towards R.F. (&)

9. Move R.F. very slightly towards L.F. (&)

10. R.F. to side, small step. (4)

10. L.F. to side, small step. (4)

Cha Cha Cha—The Basic Movement with Lady's Solo Turn Under Arm

Man

This figure consists of a Basic Movement for the Man. On the fifth step he must help the Lady to turn to her right with his right hand and then raise the joined hands and release hold with his right hand. He will then continue dancing steps six to ten of the Basic Movement while the Lady turns under the raised arms. Lower the arms and replace right hand on the Lady's back towards the end of the Chassé. Follow this figure with the Basic Movement.

Start here

1. L.F. forward. (1)
Man

1. R.F. back. (1)
Lady

2. Replace weight back to R.F. (2)

2. Replace weight forward to L.F. (2)

3. L.F. to side, small step. (3)

3. R.F. to side, small step. (3)

4. Move R.F. very slightly towards L.F. (&)

4. Move L.F. very slightly towards R.F. (&)

5. L.F. to side, small step. With right hand commence to turn Lady to her right and then release hold with right hand and raise left hand. (4)

5. R.F. to side, small step. (4)

Lady

On the fifth step of the Basic Movement the Man will release hold with his right hand and commence to turn to the right. You will now dance two forward steps turning to the right under the raised arm for almost a complete turn and then dance a Chassé to the side continuing to turn slightly to the right to end facing the Man again.

6. R.F. back, turning the Lady to her right with left hand raised high above Lady's head. (1)

6. L.F. forward, turning to the right under the raised arms. (1)

7. Replace weight forward to L.F. and continue to turn Lady to her right. (2)

7. R.F. forward, still turning to the right. (2)

8. R.F. to side, small step. Lower joined arms. (3)

8. L.F. to side, small step, still turning slightly to the right to face the Man. (&)

9. Move L.F. very slightly towards R.F. and place right hand on Lady's back. (&)

9. Move R.F. very slightly towards L.F. (4)

10. R.F. to side, small step. (4)

10. L.F. to side, small step. (5)

Cha Cha Cha—The New York

Man

In this very popular figure the Man and Lady will be side by side facing the same way on steps one, two, six and seven. Dance it after the Basic Movement releasing hold with the right hand on the last step of the latter. Repeat the figure once or twice and then take normal hold and follow with the Basic Movement.

Start here

1. L.F. forward turning a quarter to the right. (1) **Man**

1. R.F. forward turning a quarter to the left. (1) **Lady**

2. Replace weight back to R.F. (2)

2. Replace weight back to L.F. (2)

3, 4, 5. Chassé to side, L.F., R.F., L.F. turning a quarter to the left to face the Lady and take her left hand in your right hand. Release hold with left hand. (3 & 4)

3, 4, 5. Chassé to side, R.F., L.F., R.F. turning a quarter to the right to face the Man. The Man will take your left hand into his right hand and release hold of your right hand. (3 & 4)

Lady

On steps one, two, six and seven the Man and Lady will be side by side, facing the same way. The Man will release hold with his right hand before commencing the figure.

6. R.F. forward turning a quarter to the left. (1)

7. Replace weight back to L.F. (2)

8, 9, 10. Chassé to side, R.F., L.F., R.F. turning a quarter to the right to face the Lady and take her right hand in your left hand. Release hold with right hand. (3 & 4)

6. L.F. forward turning a quarter to the right. (1)

7. Replace weight back to R.F. (2)

8, 9, 10. Chassé to side, L.F., R.F., L.F. turning a quarter to the left to face the Man. The Man will take your right hand into his left hand and release hold of your left hand. (3 & 4)

Cha Cha Cha—The Time Step

This figure is danced solo by the Man and Lady and their steps are similar. First dance the Basic Movement releasing hold completely at the end of the last Chassé. Repeat the Time Step once or twice and then regain normal hold and continue into the Basic Movement.

Start here

1. Cross L.F. behind R.F. (1) **Man**
1. Cross R.F. behind L.F. (1) **Lady**

2. Replace weight to R.F. (2)
2. Replace weight to L.F. (2)

3, 4, 5. Chassé to side, L.F., R.F., L.F. (3 & 4)

3, 4, 5. Chassé to side, R.F., L.F., R.F. (3 & 4)

6. Cross R.F. behind L.F. (1)

6. Cross L.F. behind R.F. (1)

7. Replace weight to L.F. (2)

7. Replace weight to R.F (2)

8, 9, 10. Chassé to side, R.F., L.F., R.F. (3 & 4)

8, 9, 10. Chassé to side, L.F., R.F., L.F. (3 & 4)

The Samba

The bright, lilting music of the Samba makes this dance from Brazil most popular. A strong characteristic of the dance is the slight 'bouncing' movement which is used on most figures and is achieved by the bending and straightening of the knees. To practise this stand with the feet together and the knees slightly relaxed. Now straighten the knees slightly and relax them again. Say 'a' as you straighten and 'Slow' as you relax. Make the 'a' sound short, like 'er'. Repeat this several times, with the music if possible. On no account make the movement jerky. Try to feel like a balloon which is being softly bounced up and down on the floor.

Unlike the Cha Cha Cha the Samba will move round the room although there is not too much progression. The steps are not big and are taken flat unless otherwise stated in the description.

Here are some simple amalgamations to help you as you learn the figures:

1. Commence facing diagonally to the wall and dance the Basic Movement gradually turning to the right to end facing diagonally to the wall again. Dance from four to eight Basic Movements to complete the turn.

2. Having danced the Basic Movement as above go straight into the Progressive Basic Movement. Do this two or three times and then follow with the Basic Movement. If you are near a corner dance a series of Basic Movements to end facing diagonally to the wall of the next Line of Dance and continue into the Progressive Basic Movement.

3. Dance a series of Basic Movements to end facing the wall. Now step to the side into a Whisk to the Right followed by a Whisk to the Left and then repeat these two Whisks. Now step forward on the right foot into the Basic Movement.

4. Dance a series of Basic Movements to face the wall and then into three Whisks, first to the right, then to the left, then to the right again. Now turn to face the Line of Dance in Promenade Position and continue with the Walks in Promenade Position. Repeat these several times and then dance a Whisk to the Left turning a quarter to right (Lady turns a quarter to left) to face partner. Continue by stepping forward on the right foot into the Basic Movement

Samba—The Basic Movement

Man and Lady

Commence this figure in any direction in the room. You may make a gradual turn to the right if you wish, using four to eight Basic Movements to complete a full turn. Remember after each closing step to use the same foot again.

The 'bounce' action previously explained is achieved by the bending and straightening of the knees.

Start here

4. Close R.F. to L.F. without weight, slightly bending the knees, then straighten them slightly. (S)

4. Close L.F. to R.F. without weight, slightly bending the knees, then straighten them slightly. (S)

3. L.F. back, slightly bending the knees, then straighten them slightly. (S)

3. R.F. forward, slightly bending the knees, then straighten them slightly. (S)

2. Close L.F. to R.F. without weight, slightly bending the knees, then straighten them slightly. (S)

2. Close R.F. to L.F. without weight, slightly bending the knees, then straighten them slightly. (S)

1. R.F. forward, slightly bending the knees, then straighten them slightly. (S) **Man**

1. L.F. back, slightly bending the knees, then straighten them slightly. (S) **Lady**

Samba—The Progressive Basic Movement

This figure is used to progress along the side of the room. There is no turn and only very slight 'bounce'. The steps for the Man and Lady are similar.

Commence facing diagonally to the wall (Lady backing diagonally to the wall) directly following the Basic Movement. Repeat the figure once or twice and then go into the Basic Movement.

Start here

4. Close R.F. to L.F. without weight. (S)	3. L.F. to side. (S)	2. Close L.F. to R.F. without weight. (S)	1. R.F. forward. (S) Man
4. Close L.F. to R.F. without weight. (S)	3. R.F. to side. (S)	2. Close R.F. to L.F. without weight. (S)	1. L.F. back. (S). **Lady**

How's your Cha Cha Charm?

Can it get you through on its own, girls?

You can be beautiful without being charming. You can also be charming without being beautiful.

Even Anne of Cleves — one of history's more notorious battleaxes — was considered charming by those of her contemporaries who got to know her better than her husband chose to.

But her charm didn't work on Henry VIII, did it? It's on record that he flatly refused to dance with her. Her own husband, if you please.

Beauty is skin deep, they say. But how deep is skin? *Beauty* in the *Know the Craft* series tells you.

It goes a bit deeper than the 'dab of powder, hint of eye shadow and right shade of lipstick' routine.

It deals with organics as much as with beauty treatments. And what skin, eyes and hair demand from you. Not only in the way of cosmetic artistry but also in what's required to give Mother Nature a hand with fundamental conditioning.

Samba—The Whisks to Right and Left

The Whisks are danced facing the wall (Lady backing the wall) directly after the Basic Movement and once again the steps for the Man and Lady are similar.

As each Whisk consists of three steps to be fitted into two beats of music they are counted 'S a S'.

6. Replace weight to L.F. keeping it in same place and slightly bending the knees, then straighten them slightly. (S)
6. Replace weight to R.F. keeping it in same place and slightly bending the knees, then straighten them slightly. (S)

5. Cross R.F. behind L.F. on toe, right toe to left heel. Slightly straighten the knees. ('a')
5. Cross L.F. behind R.F. on toe, left toe to right heel. Slightly straighten the knees. ('a')

4. L.F. to side, slightly bending the knees. (S)

4. R.F. to side, slightly bending the knees. (S)

Take steps two and five (the crossing steps) on the toe. The other steps are all flat. Repeat the six steps and then follow with the Basic Movement.

Start here

  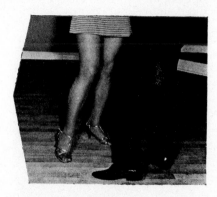

3. Replace weight to R.F. keeping it in same place and slightly bending the knees, then straighten them slightly. (S)

3. Replace weight to L.F. keeping it in same place and slightly bending the knees, then straighten them slightly. (S)

2. Cross L.F. behind R.F. on toe, left toe to right heel. Slightly straighten the knees. ('a')

2. Cross R.F. behind L.F. on toe, right toe to left heel. Slightly straighten the knees. ('a')

1. R.F. to side, slightly bending the knees. (S) **Man**

1. L.F. to side, slightly bending the knees. (S) **Lady**

Samba—The Walks in Promenade Position

Promenade Position is a position where the Man and the Lady are side by side with their bodies turned very slightly towards each other to form a V-shape, as you will see by the photographs. First dance the Whisks to Right and Left and then another Whisk to Right (steps one to three). The Man will now turn slightly to the left and the Lady slightly to the right to Promenade Position and continue with the Walks described below. Keep the feet facing the Line of Dance and move along the Line of Dance throughout the Walks. Repeat them

6. Draw R.F. back about two inches. (S)

6. Draw L.F. back about two inches. (S)

5. L.F. back on toe, small step. ('a')

5. R.F. back on toe, small step ('a')

4. R.F. forward, slightly bending the knees. (S)

4. L.F .forward, slightly bending the knees. (S)

once or twice and then the Man will turn a quarter to the right and the Lady a quarter to the left to face each other as they both step to the side to continue with a Whisk to the Left. (Steps four to six). Follow with the Whisks to the Right and Left and then the Basic Movement.

Do not lower the heel of the back foot on steps two and five. There is a very slight 'bouncing' action on the Walks.

Start here

3. Draw L.F. back about two inches. (S)

3. Draw R.F. back about two inches. (S)

2. R.F. back on toe, small step. ('a')

2. L.F. back on toe, small step. ('a')

1. L.F. forward, slightly bending the knees. (S) **Man**

1. R.F. forward, slightly bending the knees. (S) **Lady**

A Final Word

The 'International Style' of Ballroom and Latin American dancing is now recognised throughout the world as a recreation which combines artistry, movement and rhythmic interpretation. It has indeed developed into an international sport and at the present time there are at least three dozen countries in the world where national and international championships are promoted.

The absolute beginner who has studied this book will know sufficient figures to enter the Ballroom but it would be wise to attend the beginners' classes of a qualified teacher. By attending such classes beginners will gain the confidence necessary to adapt themselves to dancing with different partners and in different surroundings, with other people on the floor. The sympathetic atmosphere of a dance studio combined with the guidance of a qualified teacher will help to overcome difficulties far more quickly and certainly more pleasantly than a crowded ballroom.

Later, when practice has brought a free, flowing movement combined with good style, dancers can measure their progress by entering the amateur Medal Tests conducted by the Imperial Society of Teachers of Dancing.

The Imperial Society of Teachers of Dancing,

70 Gloucester Place, London W1H 4AJ was founded in 1904 and is a body limited by guarantee registered as an Educational Charity. The Society's main function is to issue after examination qualifications as a teacher of dancing in the various specialist techniques taught by its 8,500 members, in schools of dancing throughout the world, to maintain and improve teaching standards, and to promote knowledge of the dance.

The techniques covered are:

Ballroom dancing and its related forms of Latin American and Sequence Dancing.

Ballet (Two methods are covered namely the Cecchetti Method and the Imperial Society Syllabus).

Greek Dance (Ruby Ginner Method) and Natural Movement (Madge Atkinson Method).

National Dance (Covering European Folk and Character Dance).

Historical Dance.

Modern Dance (Embracing Jazz, Tap, and various specialist stage techniques).

Scottish Dance (Country and Highland).

In each Branch an authoritative and comprehensive Syllabus has been evolved by a committee of experts in the technique concerned and examinations are conducted in the following categories.

Grade Examinations

These are arranged in Ballet, Ballroom Dancing, Greek Dance and Natural Movement, Modern Dance, and National Dance. The syllabi vary in detail some covering 7 grades from Primary to Grade VI and others only covering grades I to III. However in every case the detailed syllabi, on which the examinations are based, guide the teacher and ensure that the pupils training is neither rushed nor scamped. A gradual development in their dance is planned so that neither bodies nor minds are strained. All teachers are, therefore, on common ground as regards standards and teaching methods; a brilliant teacher is in no way hampered, while the large body of general teachers throughout the country have a logical complete and consistent plan upon which to work.

Medal Tests

These are arranged in Ballroom Dancing and its related forms for adults and children and (almost exclusively for children) in Greek, Modern, National, and Scottish Dances. The tests encourage good style and technique and comprise Bronze, Silver, Gold, Gold Star (See picture) and higher awards. The Society has always set a high standard for its tests and examinations and the syllabi established by the Society in most techniques have been adopted by similar Organisations throughout the world, where it is recognised by those conversant with the subject that the examination standards and procedure evolved by the Society are pre-eminent.

Student and Professional Examinations

The Grade Examination syllabi provide an introduction to the student and professional examinations which will equip candidates either for a career on the stage or as teacher. On the other hand a child who has an interest in dancing without wishing to make it her profession will have acquired through the grades a supple body and a broader appreciation of dance and the theatre.

The professional examinations in the Ballroom and related Branches consist of a Student Teacher examination and then of three syllabi for Associate, Membership, and Fellowship Status within the Branch. In the other Branches covering the Theatre and Educational techniques of Ballet, Modern, and National Dance, etc., there are syllabi in three sections: Elementary, Intermediate, and Advanced. These may be taken by students from age 14 with little theoretical coverage when no status in the Society is gained. Later from age 16 they may be taken as student-teachers, when Student Membership status in the Society can be applied for. The examinations as a teacher commence at age 18 for Associate and later aged respectively 21 and 23 for Licentiate or Fellow.

General

Further information on the examinations is obtainable from the Society and a separate Syllabus is published for each Branch.

The Gold Star Award issued for Ballroom Dancing.

J. Ward, Dewsbury, England